To:

From:

This coupon book is my gift to you–the biggest chocoholic I know. These coupons never expire and are redeemable at any time by me.

The Chocoholic's

Sourcebooks, Inc.
Naperville, IL

Published by Sourcebooks Inc., P.O. Box 372, Naperville, IL 60566 (630) 961-3900 FAX: (630) 961-2168

Internal design and production by Andrew Sardina and Scott Theisen

These coupons are for entertainment purposes only—please do not attempt to redeem them at your local store. The coupons hold no monetary value and cannot be redeemed for complimentary or discounted product at any retail outlet. Neither Sourcebooks, Inc., nor these coupons are in any way associated with any trademark holders or manufacturers mentioned in this book. All brand names and product names used in this book are trademarks, registered trademarks, or trade names of their respective holders.

Printed and bound in the United States of America.

10 9 8 7 6 5 4 3 2

The Chocoholic's

C O U P O N B O O K

Chocolate fantasy
coupon! This coupon
is good for one
chocolate eclair

Personal notes _____

_____

"I confess. I will go to any lengths to obtain a particular chocolate. Even further, if more than one kind is involved."

—Adreanne Marcus

The
Chocoholic's
C O U P O N   B O O K

Chocolate chill! This coupon is good for one emergency chocolate ice cream run!

Personal notes _____

_____

Chocolate contains phenylethylamine, the same substance that occurs naturally in a person who is in love.

The Chocoholic's

C O U P O N   B O O K

Chocolate attack! This coupon is good for one impulse buy candy bar at the grocery store checkout

Personal notes _____

_____

"You know how I like to describe the way chocolate makes people feel? Watch a child devour a candy bar—that's contentment."

—Sandra Ramage

The
Chocoholic's

C O U P O N   B O O K

Emergency chocolate run! This coupon is good for one hot fudge sundae

Personal notes _____

_____

A human's "normal" temperature is 98.6° Fahrenheit—which is also the melting temperature of the cocoa butter in chocolate.

The Chocoholic's

COUPON BOOK

Chocolate bake-fest! This coupon is redeemable for one chocolate cookbook, my treat

Personal notes _____

_____

"What food do you crave? Ask the question with enough smoldering emphasis on the last word, and the answer is bound to be chocolate."

—Diane Ackerman

The Chocoholic's

C O U P O N   B O O K

Chocolate chill!
This coupon is
good for one bowl
of chocolate frozen
yogurt

Personal notes _____

_____

"If there is one flavor that can cause Americans to salivate at the mention of the name, it is chocolate."

—Craig Claiborne

The Chocoholic's
C O U P O N   B O O K

International chocoholic!
Italian chocolate! This coupon
is redeemable for one
chocolate toronne

Personal notes _____

_____

"Like the final act of a play or the crescendo of a symphony, we expect a good chocolate sweet to leave us speechless, craving for more."

—Suzanne Ausnit

The Chocoholic's

C O U P O N   B O O K

**Chocolate fantasy coupon!
This coupon is good for one
box of chocolate truffles**

Personal notes _____

_____

"Chocolate truffles are the black gold of candydom."

—Jane Salzfass Freiman

The
Chocoholic's
C O U P O N   B O O K

Chocolatey thirst!
This coupon is good
for one cup of
hot chocolate
(marshmallows
optional)

Personal notes _____

_____

"The superiority of chocolate, both for health and nourishment, will soon give it the preference over tea and coffee in America which it has in Spain."

—Thomas Jefferson

The
Chocoholic's

C O U P O N   B O O K

Chocolate fantasy coupon! This coupon is redeemable for one box of gourmet chocolates

Personal notes _____

_____

"...dark is to milk chocolate what Dom Perignon® is to Dr. Pepper®."

—Jenifer Havery Lang

The Chocoholic's

C O U P O N   B O O K

Chocolate bake-fest!
This coupon is good
for one batch of
gooey homemade
brownies

Personal notes _____

_____

"Brownies are the classic comfort food, the perfect compensation for a busy life."

—Leslie Land

The
Chocoholic's
C O U P O N   B O O K

This coupon is redeemable for one chocolate dessert at your favorite restaurant (not dinner, just dessert!)

Personal notes _____

_____

"Flowers speak the language of love for some, but for others, it's chocolate that fans the flame."

—Rebecca J. Pate

The Chocoholic's

C O U P O N   B O O K

Chocolate chill! This coupon is good for one box of Fudgsicles®

Personal notes _____

_____

Chocolate confers energy. Its active ingredients are caffeine and theobromine, both of which exert a stimulant effect on the central nervous system.

The Chocoholic's

COUPON BOOK

Chocolate fantasy coupon! This coupon is good for one creamy slice of French silk pie

Personal notes _____

_____

French silk pie was first introduced at a bake-off contest in 1952—it won first place.

The Chocoholic's

C O U P O N   B O O K

Chocolate attack!
This coupon is good
for one huge slice of
devil's food cake

Personal notes _____

_____

"I love dark, rich devil's food cake, gloriously frosted with butter-cream rosettes. So why do I shake convulsively at the mere thought of these luscious delights?"

—Cherie Baker

The Chocoholic's

C O U P O N   B O O K

International chocoholic!
German choctoberfest!
This coupon is
redeemable for one
German chocolate cake

Personal notes _____

_____

On average, Americans consume 10 pounds of chocolate a year; the average European consumes 12 pounds a year.

The
Chocoholic's
C O U P O N   B O O K

Chocolate chill! This coupon is redeemable for one gallon of chocolate ice cream (you don't have to eat it all at once!)

Personal notes _____

_____

Montezuma has been credited with being the "Father of Chocolate Ice Cream." He reportedly took snow from a volcano and poured whipped, frothy "chocolatl" over it in the early sixteenth century.

The Chocoholic's
C O U P O N   B O O K

**Chocolate fantasy coupon.
This coupon entitles you to
a copy of the Godiva®
Chocolatier© magazine**

Personal notes _____

_____

"Chocolate is downfall, happiness, pleasure, love, ecstasy, fantasy...chocolate makes us wicked, guilty, sinful, healthy, chic, happy."

—Elaine Sherman

The Chocoholic's

COUPON BOOK

Chocolate chill!
This coupon is good for
one gallon of chocolate
chip cookie dough
ice cream

Personal notes _____

_____

Cocoa beans vary considerably in taste. Each region produces a particular flavored bean. To make chocolate, different types are blended according to the wishes of the manufacturer.

The Chocoholic's

COUPON BOOK

Chocolate attack!
This coupon is good
for one stop at the
cookie store in
the mall

Personal notes _____

_____

"Research tells us that fourteen out of any ten individuals like chocolate."

—Sandra Boynton

The Chocoholic's

C O U P O N   B O O K

Chocolatey thirst!
Wash it all down with a
cold glass of milk.
Better yet, make it
chocolate milk

Personal notes _____

_____

Chocolate Notebook

M&M's® were developed in 1940 and marketed as chocolate that was easy to eat in any weather.

The Chocoholic's

In case of emergency... This coupon entitles you to keep a 3 Musketeers® bar in the freezer

Personal notes _____

_____

The original 3 Musketeers® bar of 1932 had three parts; chocolate, vanilla, and strawberry. In the 1940s it became all chocolate.

The Chocoholic's

C O U P O N   B O O K

**Chocolate fantasy coupon!
This coupon is good for
one Fannie May®
indulgence day**

Personal notes _____

_____

"Strength is the capacity to break a chocolate bar into four pieces with your bare hands—and then eat just one of the pieces."

—Judith Viorst

The Chocoholic's

C O U P O N   B O O K

Chocolate chill!
This coupon is good
for a chocolate
shake stop

Personal notes _____

_____

Each Hershey's Kiss™ is wrapped in five square inches of foil and contains 25 calories.

The Chocoholic's
C O U P O N   B O O K

International chocoholic!
French chocolate amour!
This coupon is
redeemable for one
chocolate mousse

Personal notes _____

_____

"You don't like chocolate. You don't even love chocolate. Chocolate is something you have an affair with."

—Geneen Roth

The Chocoholic's

C O U P O N   B O O K

Chocolatey thirst! This coupon entitles you to use chocolate milk in your cereal

Personal notes _____

_____

Tootsie Rolls® were invented by Leo Hirschfield, who named them after his daughter in 1896.

The Chocoholic's

C O U P O N   B O O K

**Chocoholic combos!
This coupon is good for one
bag of chocolate-covered
peanuts**

Personal notes _____

_____

Chocolate Notebook

M&M's® were part of military rations in Word War II.

The Chocoholic's
COUPON BOOK

Chocolate fantasy coupon! This coupon is good for one chocolate torte

Personal notes _____

_____

Cocoa trees grow in many parts of the world, but only within twenty degrees north and south of the equator.

The Chocoholic's
C O U P O N   B O O K

Chocolate attack!
This coupon entitles
you to eat dessert
first

Personal notes _____

_____

"Chocolate makes otherwise normal people melt into strange states of ecstasy."

—John West

The Chocoholic's

C O U P O N   B O O K

International chocoholic! English chocolate! This coupon is redeemable for one batch of toffee

Personal notes _____

_____

During the seventeenth century, England maintained a high import duty on cocoa beans—punishment for smuggling was at least one year of jail time.

The Chocoholic's
COUPON BOOK

Chocoholic combos! This coupon is good for one chocolate hazelnut biscotti with your cup of coffee

Personal notes _____

_____

"Nine out of ten people like chocolate.
The tenth person always lies."

—John G. Tullius

The Chocoholic's

C O U P O N   B O O K

Chocolate attack! This coupon entitles you to dig into a container of chocolate frosting

Personal notes _____

_____

"Although there's no pharmacological evidence that chocolate is addictive, people in thrall to the substance do goofy things."

—Judith Stone

The Chocoholic's

C O U P O N   B O O K

**Chocolate bake-fest!
This coupon is good
for one batch of
chocolate chip
cookies**

Personal notes _____

_____

Ruth Wakefield is credited for having invented chocolate chip cookies when she chopped up semi-sweet chocolate bars and added them to a batch of cookie dough.

The Chocoholic's

C O U P O N   B O O K

Chocoholic combos!
This coupon is
good for one box of
chocolate-covered
cherries

Personal notes _____

_____

"...truly wonderful masterpieces can be created with great skill and all will be acclaimed with great enthusiasm, simply because they are made with chocolate."

—Jennie Reekie

The Chocoholic's
COUPON BOOK

Chocolate attack!
This coupon is good
for one bag of
Hershey's Kisses™

Personal notes _____

_____

Nearly 30 million Hershey's Kisses™ are produced a day. The bite-sized chocolates were introduced in 1907.

The
Chocoholic's
C O U P O N   B O O K

Chocoholic combos! This coupon entitles you to use chocolate-covered bananas in your banana split

Personal notes _____

_____

"I often dreamed about picking chocolate from a chocolate tree and eating my fill."

—Maida Heatter

The Chocoholic's

C O U P O N   B O O K

Chocolatey thirst! This coupon is good for one chocolate mocha first thing in the morning

Personal notes _____

_____

"Does the notion of chocolate preclude the concept of free will?"

—Sandra Boynton

The Chocoholic's

C O U P O N   B O O K

Chocolate chill!
This coupon is
redeemable for one
gallon of Rocky Road
ice cream

Personal notes _____

_____

"Any sane person loves chocolate."

—Bob Greene

The Chocoholic's

C O U P O N   B O O K

Chocolate breakfast.
This coupon is good
for one heaping bowl
of Cocoa Krispies®

Personal notes _____

_____

Oreo® cookies were introduced in 1912, four years after Sunshine Biscuits® introduced Hydrox® cookies.

The Chocoholic's

C O U P O N   B O O K

Doctor's orders
coupon! This coupon
orders you to
eat one piece of
chocolate daily

Personal notes _____

_____

"...the best part of Easter is eating your children's candy while they are sleeping and trying to convince them the next morning that the chocolate rabbit came with one ear."

—Anna Quindlen

The Chocoholic's
C O U P O N   B O O K

Chocolate bake-fest! This coupon is good for one batch of fresh-baked chocolate chip muffins

Personal notes _____

_____

The word "chocolate" is derived from a combination of the Mayan word "xocoatl," and the Aztec word for cocoa, "cacahuatl," meaning "food of the gods."

The Chocoholic's

C O U P O N   B O O K

**International chocoholic!
Swiss chocolate! This
coupon is redeemable for a
chocolate fondue**

Personal notes _____

_____

"Giving chocolate to others is an intimate form of communication, a sharing of deep, dark, secrets."

—Milton Zelman

The Chocoholic's

C O U P O N   B O O K

Chocolate attack!
This coupon is good
for one bottle of
Hershey's® Chocolate
Syrup

Personal notes _____

_____

Chocolate Notebook

The largest producer of cocoa beans for commercial purposes is Ghana, Africa.

The
Chocoholic's

C O U P O N   B O O K

Chocolate theater! This coupon entitles you to one viewing of *Willy Wonka and the Chocolate Factory*.

Personal notes _____

_____

Daniel Peter of Switzerland is credited with perfecting a solid milk chocolate bar for eating in 1875.

The
Chocoholic's
C O U P O N   B O O K

Chocolate relaxation
coupon. This coupon
entitles you to recline on
the couch and enjoy
some chocolate
bon-bons

Personal notes _____

_____

Chocolate Notebook

The first Whitman's Samplers® were introduced in 1912.

The Chocoholic's

Chocolate chill! This coupon is good for one chocolate brownie ice cream sundae

Personal notes _____

_____

Mature cocoa trees reach a height of twenty to twenty-five feet.

The Chocoholic's

C O U P O N B O O K

**Chocolate fantasy coupon!
This coupon is good for one
rich chocolate tart**

Personal notes _____

_____

"*Chocolate, of course, is the stuff of which fantasies are made.*"

—Judith Olney

The Chocoholic's

C O U P O N   B O O K

**Chocolatey thirst!
This coupon is
redeemable for one
bottle of Yoo-Hoo®
chocolate drink**

Personal notes _____

_____

The Nestle Company introduced Nestle's Crunch® in 1938 and chocolate chips, Toll House Morsels®, in 1939.

The
Chocoholic's
C O U P O N   B O O K

Chocolate attack!
This coupon entitles
you to put chocolate
syrup on everything!

Personal notes _____

_____

Chocolate Notebook

An average of 600,000 tons of cacao beans are consumed each year.

The Chocoholic's

C O U P O N   B O O K

Chocoholic combos!
This coupon is good
for one chocolate-
covered granola bar

Personal notes _____

_____

"My desire for chocolate has seldom abated, even in times of great peril."

—Marcel Desaulniers

The
Chocoholic's
C O U P O N   B O O K

Emergency chocolate run!
This coupon entitles you to a trip
to Baskin-Robbins®

Personal notes _____

_____

Aging develops flavor in dark chocolate in much the same way good red wine improves with age.

The Chocoholic's
COUPON BOOK

Chocolate relaxation coupon. This coupon entitles you to curl up with a good book and a box of chocolate

Personal notes _____

_____

"It soothes both stomach and brain, and for this reason, as well as for others, it is the best friend of those engaged in literary pursuits."

—Baron Justus von Liebig

The Chocoholic's
C O U P O N B O O K

International chocoholic!
Mexican chocolate fiesta!
This coupon is
redeemable for one
chicken mole

Personal notes _____

_____

The Mexican Indians included cacao beans in their ceremonies as a reminder of the gift that had been left them by their god, Quetzalcoatl.

The Chocoholic's
COUPON BOOK

Chocolate attack!
This coupon is good
for one plate of fudge

Personal notes _____

_____

Chocolate Notebook

In the early 1900s, fudge was often cooked over gaslight as an excuse for collegiate parties after "lights-out."

The Chocoholic's

C O U P O N   B O O K

Chocolate chill! This coupon entitles you to chocolate sprinkles on your next bowl of ice cream

Personal notes _____

_____

"Chocolates reflect the tastes of those who buy them."

—Adreanne Marcus

The Chocoholic's

COUPON BOOK

In case of emergency...
This coupon is good for one bag of
chocolate chips. Eat 'em straight
outta the bag!

Personal notes _____

_____

There are approximately 675 chocolate chip morsels in each 12-oz. bag of chocolate chips.

The
Chocoholic's

C O U P O N   B O O K

Chocolate attack! This coupon is good for one giant bowl of chocolate pudding

Personal notes _____

_____

The Aztecs believed that chocolate conferred universal wisdom and knowledge to thank those who drank it.

The Chocoholic's

C O U P O N   B O O K

International chocoholic! Arctic chocolate! This coupon is good for one chilly Eskimo Pie®

Personal notes _____

_____

Chocolate Notebook

"Eskimo Pie®" was patented by Christian Nelson in January 1922.

The Chocoholic's
C O U P O N   B O O K

Chocolate vacation!
This coupon is good
for one weekend
visit to Hershey,
Pennsylvania

Personal notes _____

_____

"For some reason or other, a Hershey's® bar would save my soul right now."

—Jack Kerouac, *The Dharma Bums*

The Chocoholic's

C O U P O N   B O O K

Chocolate attack!
This coupon is good
for one Mississippi
Mud Pie

Personal notes _____

_____

"If in fact you are what you eat I am a 114-pound bar of bittersweet chocolate."

—Lora Brody

Send us your coupon idea!

What do you most want to give the chocoholic in your life? Chocoholic's, what do you really want from your loved ones? Send us your coupon ideas—if we use them in our next book or in future editions, we'll send you a free copy of the finished book! Submission of ideas implies free and clear permission to use in any and all future editions. Send your coupons to:

Sourcebooks
Attn: Coupon Ideas
P.O. Box 372
Naperville, IL 60566

My Ideas

Other great coupon books from Sourcebooks

I Love You Mom Coupons
I Love You Dad Coupons
Golf Coupons
Love Coupons, by Gregory J.P. Godek, author of *1001 Ways to Be Romantic*
The Best of Friends Coupons
Happy Birthday Coupons
My Favorite Teacher Coupons
Merry Christmas Coupons

These titles and other Sourcebooks publications are available now at your local book or gift store, or by calling Sourcebooks at (630) 961-3900.